Praise for *The Opposite of Cruelty*

"Steven Leyva's *The Opposite of Cruelty* reads like a series of odes and vignettes praising the very fact of daily Black life. Each poem is careful to move that which is mundane to a position of praise, from the right amount of salt necessary for making grits to worms who 'perform their transubstantiation / through the fragile dark.' Witty, ambitious, and formally inventive, *The Opposite of Cruelty* is a beautiful book."
—**Jericho Brown,** *The Tradition*, winner of the Pulitzer Prize

"These poems break the conventions of time and place to make a map of family here and on the other side of here. Leyva makes a map for a son, reminding him to 'keep your heart.' These poems ask, 'What would the world be / if it had you instead of your legacy?' And in answer, we, the reader and the poet, make art, a life, a home. Reading *The Opposite of Cruelty* is like listening to a mix of Charles Mingus, Nina Simone, and Outkast while setting fire to the world's most famous maps."
—**Tyree Daye,** *a little bump in the earth* and *Cardinal*

"Steven Leyva's newest book, *The Opposite of Cruelty*, is full of lyrics that pack more music and thinking into one line than many poets pack into a whole poem. Here are expansive, tensile sonnets that explore the fragility and intensity of joy, that sing the praises of both ancient myth and popular culture, that meld the devotional to the political. Here are odes and aubades, here are poems that playfully reinvent poetic form in order to question the constructions (and restrictions) we've used to socially imagine race. This is a generous, beautiful collection that speaks directly about how and what we choose to love in this dazzling, changeable, sometimes frightening world."
—**Paisley Rekdal,** *West: A Translation*

"I've admired Steven Leyva's poems for as long as I've been lucky to call him my friend, and his second collection, *The Opposite of Cruelty,* makes it easy to remember why: he is a poet of compassionate eye and generous spirit, who braids music and rigorous thought into each of his carefully textured lines with aplomb. In these odes and aubades, self-portraits and pastorals, sonnets both broken and doubled, Leyva merges the devotional and political, the historical and personal so adeptly we can feel what we understand: they are inseparable. I recognize in this fine collection a poet in full possession of his gifts, who praises the world despite the world and sings to us of its complex and unexpected beauty. So that when the poet asks, early in the collection, 'why do I bother / to slash and slash and slash / white from this page?' I hear the unspoken answer: *to love.*"
—**Charif Shanahan,** author of *Trace Evidence: poems*

"Leyva's voice breaks through the surface of daily life to give us the depth of origin, place, history, and music. His second collection, remarkable for embracing lyricism, narrative, and political consciousness, is a homecoming into childhood, fatherhood, and one's responsibility to live kindly in the erratic world. Whether in Baltimore or in New Orleans, he draws his rhythms and metaphors from life's fleeting passages, wrestling with what it means to recognize and record their beauty. The book emphasizes Leyva's range—he is a poet of cities, of fleeting time, a love poet, a friend poet, a father poet, a community poet, which is to say, a historian of the American heart."

—**Valzhyna Mort,** *Music for the Dead and Resurrected*

THE OPPOSITE
OF CRUELTY

THE OPPOSITE OF CRUELTY

Poems by Steven Leyva

BLAIR

Printed in the United States of America

Cover design by April Leidig
Cover art: "Tethered" by Karo Duro
Interior design by April Leidig

Blair is an imprint of Carolina Wren Press.

The mission of Blair/Carolina Wren Press is to seek out, nurture, and promote literary work by new and underrepresented writers.

We gratefully acknowledge the ongoing support of general operations by the Durham Arts Council's United Arts Fund and the North Carolina Arts Council.

Library of Congress Cataloging-in-Publication Data
Names: Leyva, Steven, 1982– author.
Title: The opposite of cruelty : poems / Steven Leyva.
Description: Durham : Blair, 2025.
Identifiers: LCCN 2024036306 (print) | LCCN 2024036307 (ebook) |
    ISBN 9781958888346 (paperback) | ISBN 9781958888452 (ebook)
Subjects: LCGFT: Poetry.
Classification: LCC PS3612.E997 O67 2025 (print) | LCC PS3612.E997 (ebook) |
    DDC 811/.6—dc23/eng/20240812
LC record available at https://lccn.loc.gov/2024036306
LC ebook record available at https://lccn.loc.gov/2024036307

CONTENTS

III | PIG-HEADED LIGHT

For my family
and for anyone who can
imagine a healed world

Beauty — be not caused — It Is —
Chase it, and it ceases —

—Emily Dickinson

A Poem Avoiding Its Own Tour of Force

I could begin with the slate roof of sunset
the smog has given us, or the low growl

in the throat of a window—the A/C unit
exasperated. I could begin with the cold

color of gun metal, the aria of the bullet:
sing a song full of the faith that the dark

past has taught us. I could begin in ocean:
the gray headstones of dead coral, the only

grave markers. Or approach the starting line
of seashore: the eye is colonized first. Or fire

the ceramics in our language. What name
does the sculpture give to the clay

when it lives in the kiln
of a closed mouth? I could annunciate *Fear not*

better than any angel and begin with the gray
snow on a rosebush: the promise of color. I

could begin with the wheat we sow in ether,
or the menagerie of jailed poets: Pen Pen Pen.

I could begin in doubt *true to our God, true*
to our native land. I could begin in error:

I don't care what anyone else thinks.
I could begin where I will end, in Ithakas

so gray when one speaks their name
Baltimore will be the only word anyone hears.

I could praise the present tense and begin again.
I could condition this vow: I will not love

anyone else, but instead begin to hum
in your ear, reader, lover, gray stranger.

Here Is a Sea We Cannot Call Sea

I was grown on the Gulf. Its half-moon
surf stretched from Delta to the shin
bone of Texas—Brownsville!—then

beyond, creasing into the Yucatan's slight grin
resolving in stone on stone, ruins
when a tourist says Tulum.

I was raised in an old fortress of cliffs
guarding the last syllables of an ocean's blind ode.
This toothless mouth, this salt washed memory,

pre-Columbian awe, becomes a parabola
of family taken up by land. No matter which
myths you pick, it's an immigrant's path.

I was San Pedro Sula and Ab Ovo,
New Orleans and home. The Gulf held the shape
of a bent bow. Barrier islands. Wild light and lotion.

Everyone browning like butter. Horizon frying
the onion-white sails. We travel proud
with only the fricative of our gods,

fathers, mothers, and cradlelands
unpronounceable across the border. Calin
then Carlos, then Charles, then anemic waves.

THE UNITED FRUIT COMPANY

Dawn, bright as teeth biting night's black tongue
lifts the bloodshot eyes of the shift boss, hungover
and sore as a thigh after a night of bachata on rum.

Suavemente across the shoulders
a *morena*'s kiss—every kind of digression—
clears his eyes enough to see my grandfather

harvesting bananas with a shotgun and a song
that refuses to go limp in the air. *Don Miguel,*
the boss shouts, confusing two different honorifics.

Granddad just keeps singing and shooting. By midday
he has outsung the morning insects and the shift

boss has given up, written a discharge note and small pension check—
a little seed money, a little insanity, a little uneaten fruit.

Self-Portrait as Prince of the Fire Nation

I won't ignore the obvious. The scar grows
like a new world atlas: my face conquered
and unconquered by my father's bent
fire. Annually I visit the prison
of his disappointment; the bored guards
of memory perform a cursory search,
and find him powerless, but still angry.

Anger is the mise-en-scène all the men
of my family perform in. We fire up
our baritones and loud talk our regret. We
all have mouths without enough room
for our teeth. We pretend to the calm
of jasmine tea. So few of us can redirect
lightning away from our hearts. Selah
like the sigh of a dying flame.

Perhaps I find little honor in searching
my father's face for my own. Given
this blackening scar, stretching
like an explorer's finger touching a map,
I breathe as the dragons breathe.

Seasonal Depression

Give the termites your worry / about affording the rent. They too / are saying, *eat / the rich*. Two kids up / the block slash a neighbor's tires / while the elderly / couple are away at a wedding. Why / do I even bother to tell / anyone who's listening / that everyone involved was white / except me? Give the newborn / mosquitos their banquet of blood and your worry / about diabetes and rotted teeth. Who can say / what insectivore / is waiting / to eat the things that eat / your worry. Joy: the long-tongued sloth / or joy: the pitcher / plant. Given the insistence on phoenix your tendons return to / given the moles that arrive / on your neck / year after / year from your grandmother / given the fact / that every elegy fails / to reach its true audience / why do I bother / to slash and slash and slash / white from this page?

Gorgoneion: Ft. Worth

From the snake-haired interstate
exit ramps, the city throws its stone
heart. Burnt grass cleaves the clay
embedded lawns, as sprinklers rise at 3 a.m.
dreaming the nymphs of insects: none
bigger than the dragonfly that flits
like the flint of an arrowhead that can't choose
whom to kill. My mother will retire here and live

through two botched hip replacements. There are stones
where her joints should be. She drives a big-body
SUV to floss these split tongues of concrete
and praise God and tithe her last hisses
of middle age to brass collection plates.

Here the desert and the great plateaus
and the waste of water parks insist
they are no gorgons. How useless would
Perseus be here, winged mount or not, unable
to admit he loves a mask and head. And still
the city speaks of the worthy and the unworthy.

An American Sonnet for Johnson, VT

—After Wanda Coleman

After a plain day a local bar sings
two songs: *beer and revelry* (bump then spill
like a meet-cute). Lamoille valley all
a hum. River's bow and vibrato brings

the valley close to cello, counterpoint
against the mid-'90s grunge and gain. Bar door
propped open. Distortion in a mine worker's
lungs—his curse for Mt. Belvidere tangled

in maple sap—echoes in Algonquian
We all get the afterlife we deserve.
Painters cross the Pearl Street Bridge, still flush in
gestures of drink and linseed oil, to slip

brushstrokes of sex across summer air, for which
there are two songs: come hither and Hell nah.

Arriving at College Station

Adolescent, unstylish, and wild
                 as a screwtape, most of us
had just scratched off
the lottery of sixteen unaware of our luck, smelling

ourselves in white tees,
                 in Polo boots, we arrived
on the campus of Texas A&M,
Aggie maroon bruising the buildings, the dirt,

whatever it touched. We had
                 been on a step team, a clean dozen,
for a year, pretending
to be men, brothers, gents, lovers of a grind. Look,

tenderness was about as far
                 from us as Alpha Centauri,
and the co-eds altered our orbit—
brown thighs shuttling those miniskirts. Our mouths

dropping oblong. We soaked
                 through matching baby-blue
sweaters at the after-party,
the uniform of youth hanging loose around our shoulders.

O, how we hesitated
                 to travel the light-years
between lust and love. O,
                    how the dark unraveled.

I Know You're Not a Pimp, But Pimp Remember What I Taught You

"Int'l Players Anthem" arrives on the static
free FM, that opening "So . . ." reminiscent
of *Beowulf* in translation. I turn from this
Baltimore side street, the car grinding to bones

as if the gnarled road were Grendel
ravenous, I turn to my son, tell him round
Andre 3000's quirky tenor, *keep your heart.*
No need to invent new monsters.

Like initiates at the altar
of Black ubiquity, we anoint our foreheads
so one day, he can go to a wedding and sing
I choose you, effortlessly, like everyone else.

Or maybe amend the atmosphere ripped
by America's kennings on every census.

Self-Portrait as Insect Song

I've lived as a cricket on the follicles of graves in ruined gardens. I've sat and sang before leaping into autumn's patchwork air, and it hasn't made a bit of difference. I own a yard and small house with a basement invaded by crickets. Some folks see a vacant home and treat it the same as an unmarked grave. Any fool can tell the difference between the crickets mating and a police siren. I am sure crickets do not conjure continuously the particular scissors of a bluebird's beak or what it might be to live forever, perched and afraid, without being eaten. Not everyone is an egg on a ledge. The egg of a police siren, grateful for its bramble of color, hasn't any ordinary black snake to make its nest ruinous. And still, the air suffers its song. Nature cannot commit to its own savagery.

Another Incident

—After Countee Cullen

My mother visits Baltimore to help us remember
why she will never move here. The cold & blood
pressure. Her mother who we buried last fall
is summoned in small talk and feckless hush

over stone grits sitting in a saucepan. No one
will bother to clean it for weeks.
She grabs a whole fist of salt and throws it
like a last rite into the pan. *Not enough*

she half hums through a knitted muffler.
She pokes out her tongue and drums
the dusted hardwood floors. Her
mother was determined to leave

nothing to inherit. Took her yellow-bone
into the ground with her keen sense
of smell. Her mother let the termites
have the house, let the banks

have the rest, except the expired
medication in the cabinets—
God only knows where that's gone.
The marrow of chimneys

still lifts an incense her mother
would call the musk of the cross
burning. My mother lets an infection have
her finger—swollen like a styed eye.

This is all she will remember of her time
in old Baltimore, in December, before the first frost
had grown into her cerebellum, before we began
to account for what we'd lost to a season of gout.

Gates / Unsignified

*i*** has no true synonyms. So
it leaves each mouth irreplaceable
like a tooth. Perhaps there are still
mysteries, but how will
they be known? Your parents
fill out forms, and that name
is yours. Friends pull from fog
stolen sobriquets that are your way
to skip out of those forms. Still: *i***.

Self-Portrait in a Hand-Me-Down Shirt

—After Robert Hayden

The latitudes on my t-shirts, these
perfectly loose blues and whites,
venetian blinds, spotless as the Chuck
Taylors my father prized. My feet

in legacy. The carpet, an unrelaxed tongue,
curls in photographer's kitsch,
my knee bent like an obtuse triangle,
my half smile in denouement. My brother's

name written on the tag touching my back.
What did I know of school portraits
and the hypotenuse of loneliness? What beauty
at seven years old, reposed in me with laces

unknotted, lips closed? A slap bracelet
in my back pocket. Each eyebrow raptured.

A Perichoresis

In the South we raise a Godhead
through questioning
What city, what ward, what street?

Houston: a midwife, a first kiss, a celibate sky
New Orleans: my father and mother return
Baltimore: an endless bay that carries my son

or another way to say any port
in the storm, or that flood is a lingua franca
What block, what house, what room?

What you want isn't a darker roux
What you want isn't for me to stir
the Atlantic like a cast-iron pot, making a Gulf

Halo
A Corona Pastoral

I.

The accordion of icicles has paused its torch song
and the snow-blind cardinal sings the red from its back

into the dawn's plaintive daylight, which rubs a thumb across
the sagging gutters of row homes and alleys without considering
a single lily. What is cruel here? No favor given to the green hills
scratching the belly of Cumberland, Maryland. Abandoned mills

kick in their sleep like dreaming dogs. No meritocracy
can save Ellicott City from another flood. The Orioles'
off-season has all of Baltimore in a beer glass. Does anyone remember
the name of the last mayor sent to jail? At the car wash

down the block, graffiti separates one water from another. O God
of the voided year, of the indifferent sunlight, give us
the daily bread of quarantine: the longing to be touched
by a letter in the mail, the bald cry in the bathroom, the music of snow.

2.

By a letter in the mail, the bald cry in the bathroom, the music of snow,
love has learned its last arpeggio. What good is it to sing
in the empty amphitheater of winter? And yet the sparrow drags the diva

of spring back again. Encore after encore. The blue jays evicting the other
birds from a hollowed-out gourd, the inconsistent applause of cookware
coaxed from the back of a cabinet, the exhaust fan whistling a round. Love

is a chord we cannot pluck out of morning air. Not alone. Every instrument
must be touched, held aloft on the crown of a shoulder, kissed, or left mute.
An old tabula rasa of bay windows manifests our breath, asking, *Won't you
write your name?* Anything to be touched. The chime of notifications

no one confuses for a love song, but notice the sincere chorus of crocus
accompanying the crepe myrtle in the yard, and the stubborn rosemary
bullying the garden, and the scrape of the postal truck weighed with late mail,
all these altars burning in our eyes. Look at how much we don't know about loneliness.

3.

All these altars burning in our eyes. Look at how much. We don't know about loneliness
sought. Cities no longer coughing on SUVs. *Let me clear my throat*. The ringlet
of lampposts on Main Street as useless as a rosebush in winter. The *Sold Out* signs
hanging on the grocery shelves. *Give me a break*. The land makes a hymn
without lyrics. No sense in mumbling. Shenandoah sung like a ghost of hallelujah
in the praise the Potomac negotiates. Every kind of hum arrives on the bones
of derelict bridges below Harper's Ferry. Rust by any other name.

The dead stars hang like a DJ's poster saying *Coming Soon*. And the turntables
of sun and moon scratch the sky's vinyl. How can we not dance
in the kitchen alone, making toast, frying an egg? Every day we are searching
for the perfect outfit, a few fly boots, a coat that won't quit, to enter the club
of memory, slipping the bouncer a twenty-dollar bill from our childhood. The petty cash
begged at a parent's knee. Anticipation. The fear of walking home empty-handed
after asking for a lover's number. The deft touch of a porch light across the cheek.

4.

After asking for a lover's number, the deft touch of a porch light across the cheek
is like horizon's blushing grin in the daily aubade of dawn. Amen.

After asking for a lover's number, the deft touch of a porch light across the cheek
is like the anglerfish, whose luminosity and ugliness coexist. Amen.
After asking for a lover, number the deft touches of a porch light across the cheek.
Is there enough to fill the wolf's mouth and see what it eats? Amen,
after asking for a lover's number. The deft touch. A porch light across the cheek
is like any other kiss. Tender but never enough. Shameless. Amen.
After asking for a lover, number each deft touch. A porch lights. Across a cheek-
bone so high it forms a balcony for birthmarks, heat leaps at your palm. Amen.
After asking for a lover's number, the deft touch. A porch lights across a cheek
like a borrowed Zippo. Flash and then gone with the scent of faux Chanel. Amen

after asking for a lover's number, the deft touch of a porch light across the cheek
curves summer into the shape of an apple. Still, there is curse enough for every amen.

5.

Curves. Summer. The shape of apples. Still, a curse breaks. Every amen
uttered is a sign of hunger. Simple weight. But what of the stem we twist and discard,

what of the core made svelte by teeth, what of the seeds black as coal briquette,
what of the skin barely holding in its sweet, what of the heat of cider, what of the disobedience

required to know anything, what of the evenings alone hanging overripe in the air,
what of being put in a barrel, what of enduring the press, what of the hesitancy to blush?

Who can answer for a season of being disposable? What of the willingness to rot,
What of the hospitals brimming like an untended orchard? Simple. *Go and ferment*,

August announces. *Go and caramel yourself,* September shouts back. Take a photo
synthesis back to its source. The nerve of the Sun, the laziest God of all, to go on shining,

while a whole year's plans have fallen underfoot, like forgotten apples.
And what of returning to the earth? *Fuck it,* says the worm. *I can eat anywhere.*

Yes, worm, and feed the fish that make a miracle of replication, as the days do
cruelly. Isn't there another way to know that we need one another?

6.

Cruelty isn't there. Another way to know that we need one another
to live: My son eager to fry an egg for his sister, or he and I playing chess
for the first time. *I'm no good at this,* he says, slumping his cheek in his hand
like a mandarin orange in a ramekin. Slip. Sweep. The board astonished

and clean. We bust up. Obsolete high-school dance moves scuffing
the kitchen floor. The kids unimpressed, and having never seen *The Wiz,*
circle like crows. *You Can't Win.* Easy, now. Am I too early to every elegy?
My wife lifts a half grin watching the kids pretending to sing karaoke

while a sleeve of macarons evaporates like mist. How did we manage
to fix a leaking fridge and a basement light socket by the grace of YouTube?
And this is the easiest of our questions. We don't talk of the third day
without water my mother endured in Texas. What is the opposite of cruelty?

We scrub our teeth with any comfort: coffee, laughter, an illuminated text.
If not comfort, then the common sense of beauty.

7.

If not comfort, then common sense. Beauty
shifts its weight like a grifter meeting a mark. Soon
we will pull up the gaffer's tape from all our impromptu
stages: the hobbies we started, the friends we blocked
with our bay window curtains, the tomatoes that refused
to grow, the small district of new stretch marks on our bellies.
And the counsel of cold weather will come back
with its banal advice, Baltimore streets wilding with holiday
music once again. The recycling trucks running on time, slapping
their polyrhythms among the mourning doves. The mosquitos
either dead or mourning. The crepe myrtle in the yard nodding yes.
We account for what we've lost by cooking the ledger. We wake
to touch the thermostat remembering an infant's foot. Conductor's baton.
The accordion of icicles stretches its torch song.

That Beauty is not, as fond men misdeem,
An outward show of things, that only seem;
. . .
But that fair lamp, from whose celestial ray
That light proceeds, which kindleth lover's fire,

—Edmund Spenser

Double Sonnet Instead of an Introduction

Instead of your name, the barista writes *Eden*
across the flat white you drink and you drink
hours after the yawn of daybreak has closed
its mouth. And what of it? Error, as you well
know, began the new world. Your ancestors
shifted the vowels of your surname: an *i*
giving way to *y*. The whirr of a milk frother.

Nearly every continent is in your genealogy:
You are Black. You come from a Creole
so old no one can skin the pear of your first
language. The whole of the Gulf rests
in your spit. You are Afro-Latino and know
so little Spanish. Shame scratches its forehead
when you speak or don't speak. Seven

great-uncles named for conquistador resistors.
Two great-aunts named for precious stones.
Onyx in one eye. Jade in the other. You worship
differently than your Catholic grandparents.
Raised in a tune-up of a Black organ, you shout.
Your last name derives from Levi. The fricatives
of priesthood and Torah are all that are left. Your son

can climb one branch up the family tree and see
Scotland and Germany. His middle name is Japanese.
What even is a race? Confetti after the parade.
Night cuts its King cake into dawn, but dawn
doesn't arrive. Your mother throws a fistful of nutmeg
into the béchamel, but y'all cannot stop
arguing over what is white.

The Beauty of the Galleria

I.

The eucharist of a five-dollar bill, you eat
off the value menu at the mall's McDonalds.

Priests have their frocks and a poor kid
his oversized, hand-me-down Izod shirt,

and some thin-soled Reeboks, and oh-so
torn Levis. Equal vestments. It's Advent season,

after all, and the mall has resurrected the indoor ice-rink
for another year, and you've abandoned asking your friends,

Who bothers to learn to ice-skate in Houston? No matter,
your goal is the discount rack at Banana Republic,

its rotunda of half off, knowing you've got less
than a twenty left in your wallet. Somehow this

isn't as embarrassing as window-shopping or asking
the fine cashier in Chuck Taylors for her phone number.

In middle school your first dates slid here, just walking
around to holiday music and the brief glint of a trinket

flashing on a kiosk like a Bic lighter in the palm of a chain-
smoker. You came here to stop signifying *Goodwill*

with all of two tens you begged from your father
for which he filled his thimble of patience with ire.

2.

A classmate you know well wears so much Ralph Lauren
his nickname is Polo. Or Polo Bear to his girlfriend

who you sat behind in French class, crushing
and saying *pas du tout* when asked if you understood.

Might as well say it was Shannan, since not one of them
resides on the south side like you do, and they have

their own malls over in the north. But none like the Galleria,
where to sit on a bench outside of Saks Fifth Avenue

finishing a small fry and a Coke is the only sacrament
you can muster. And you believe if you wait long enough

someone will play Whitney Houston's "Joy to the World"
and you'll remember to save enough for bus fare,

and you won't mind the one shirt you found for ten bucks
or the turtleneck you left on the rack.

Aubade for Nuit #1

Sunrise burst in like an angry lover
packed its things in a trunk of fog
and escaped into gossip for days.

You said, *Fuck off*, steaming the apartment window
your thigh pristine with sweat instead of sunlight
and I thought that curse was for the eye

of heaven, not the swaying drunks
gawking on the cobblestone street below.
What darkness filled the night's yawn

did not wholly give way as we closed lips
around wizened mugs of coffee. All the x's
had fallen off the calendar, and we sat

naked on the kitchen floor, two days married
laughing at obtuse angles of our fumbled sex.
Under your breath you said, *How do teenagers*

do it? and I had no answer, so we laughed
again, and watched men vomit and walk
unwittingly into the sky's discarded nightshirt.

Ode to the Letter S

—After Aracelis Girmay

Split heart, you miracle worker—
having the last

word, you multiply
fish & loaves, Jesus

can't hardly compete. Boomerang
turning back to see the beginning

& end of each sentence.
S, to say you, I can't escape

the hiss of a snake:
you will not surely die.

You asymmetry passing, without
you the insistence of every slap

lapses, each sore is so metal, any steam
plays well with others.

You slanging letter, you colonizer of c.
First of my name, standing in the gap

between r/t—so, so, so what?
O, O, O is how it would be, we

would be telling all the truth
but telling it slant—& nobody

seriously wants that. I is what it is
because you stick around. Stay

tuned, says the sunset. Prince sibilant,
sovereign plurality, the slide in glissando

you set of broken handcuffs, you
incomplete infinity, you open secret.

Ode to Storm, Goddess, Thief, Mutant, Queen

Ororo, Ororo is the palindrome that saved me

Born among the misfit '80s, the too poor to be punk '80s,
I read reprints of Giant Size X-Men and recognized

the difference between a toll and a token. Fly,
shock, cool breeze, hail, maelstrom, so versatile

was my worship of controlled weather, it was
no secret I was in love with her life before deity:

lifting wallets in Cairo (need we even mention Dickens)
for the Shadow King. Claustrophobia was on the same helix

as her X-gene. I, too, feared the matchbox apartments
we crammed ourselves in. Dreaming of being bused

to a magnet school. Gifted on the floor of the X-mansion
and gifted all over my elementary transcripts. Tempest of expectations.

Ororo, Ororo is the palindrome that saved me

Ode to Static

—For Dwayne McDuffie

Look, it was nice to know
Urkel wasn't the only choice we had

in our orbit. Another Black nerd with covalent
cool we could share, a diasporic subatomic

dap, we loved you like Rakim verse
vibing every Walkman on the block. Static,

even your government name said classic
guide: Virgil Hawkins. We were in the dark

woods of spinner racks, mostly in a blizzard
of Ubermensch pulping the newborn '90s pages.

And there you were, floating on a trash can lid,
unashamed, spitting game to fine sistas

like the glow up of Oscar the Grouch. O blue
bodysuit and fitted cap. O gold overcoat

like a return of the Mack. A look 3 Stacks
might sport on an album cover. You were out

saving citizens in style. Uptown fades slicked
every head. We understood the buzz

of a tape rewinding of only being
mentioned in the news via mugshot,

so we sought other panels, comic books, the mirror
you held up to our future. Static you were a milestone

for kids like me, whose brown skin
ran the whole gamut of electro-spectrum.

Early Sunlight, Broken Summer, Buttery Day

—After Tim Seibles

Does Bruce Wayne ever wake early
                    in afternoon's velour of sunlight
                                  begging his butler for more broken
                  biscuits and tea, a hinted summer
tincture turning with the sun's buttery
                  laughter, those uncowled hours, called day?

Or is he ashamed and early
                  to the cave which suffers sunlight
                                only when some collapse leaves broken
                  his perpetual umbra, his invincible summer
laboratory. He knows his buttery
                  playboy buffooning is a costume every day.

In this cosplay he mimics early
                  Sherlock Holmes hiding in plain sunlight
                                more confining than any cave. Broken
                  bones reset, repaired each summer
winter, spring, and fall. Always buttery
                  toast uneaten. Nightstand cold. Gothic day.

Is the Batman the one waking early
                  to read poetry by dew and daylight
                                on the off chance with a riddle broken
                  a joke crumbled, and the two faces of summer
someone can be saved without a fist, buttery
                  moonlight, and fear? Those uncowled years called day.

Taiki Bansei

—For the Karasuno Boys Volleyball Team

Curious: lacquer
soaked hardwood and sneaker yawp.
Any early morning volleyball court

could be a hermit's mountain bedroom.
Which of the gods mortared the air
with humidity, and which made the doldrums

of schooldays? Animated boys hit *nice
kills* above the net. The libero
wears a hipster's shirt; the screen

printed kanji translates a cliché:
great talent matures late. The other
boys call him great guardian as he dives

again and again on the floor—
he must parry the blows, since he is
forbidden to attack. *Cover, Cover, Cover*

Curious: unrestrained
some envy curdles in me
to rip off that shirt, reach in midstream,

undress that boy's art as if one could
disrobe an animation cel and make it
manifest its cotton-poly pixels IRL.

I'd clothe a son with great talent
and late maturity, instead of a fallow
field of good behavior or a prefecture

of false self-assuredness or better yet
a boundless volleyball court without a net,
nothing to hit, nothing to kill over.

Predatory

Is this your king-
fisher, belted to a moss-
sleeved branch, its beak stuffed
with locust and honeyed fog
from the dawn? Who needs the heroic
couplets of rain and melancholy
when a full belly, orange and round
as a jawbreaker, reminds the ancestors
to stop hovering, for once, and to speak
plainly of which obscured snake
will lift its harlequin of diamonds.

N.O. Star in Vinyl Overlay on a Drowned Living Room Floor

The great storm dulls its incantations. Can any
fallen aster return? The constellations shrug off many.

This one remains, like Prometheus, pecked
apart, shat on. Even the sutures of dawn are wrecked,

and do little to mend the embarrassment
looking up through a roofless house. Indigent

dust wags its tail in the light above
a granite floor. Only a mocking love

heard in church bells clearing the throat
of the wind. If there is a fault here, spokes

of accusation, it rests below the foundations.
This city always begs to add another parish to the nation

of Atlantis. The heavens have an old swindle:
flood as judgment. Grandma can't reach her spindle

and thread. The termites have come as independent
contractors. My family home is gone. The sky refuses to repent,

like any good blues riff. Wasted prayers. The storm
has an eye where its navel should be. It performs

like a missing tooth, whistling about loss, blacking
out from a swift roundhouse, seeing stars. Lacking

the will to move on, I stand on a granite slab—was it
our living room?—the echoes of dominoes quit,

cousins' voices stir with the crickets and streetcars. Cursing
has lost its magic, but we do it anyway, conversing

in blue. *Funky-ass Katrina* fucking up a whole
generation of wealth, yah heard me. A hard luck soul

singing its un-leveed hymn through the Crown
Royal whiskey: What do they do, those who don't drown?

Early Morning Fade

The barber's knuckles brush the highest ridge
of your cheekbone. His tenderness can reach

you, like a rose petal landing in an untroubled
pool in Bethesda. The heel of his palm

cradles the clippers as if a baby
doll were held there, too small to be real;

too important to put down. He fusses over an edge-line,
before handing you a mirror. What do you say to yourself?

Immemorial

I can't decide which is more
unforgiving: history or memory. Neither
is a quicksand, neither is a sea.
I've erased a line that begins
I can't remember so often, it's breathing
palimpsest. Being whispered awake
by whatever lashes of dawn refuse
to blink or self-flagellate: lovers' names return
and fade like a cold sore. The Mid-Atlantic
coast curled into an abandoned smile. The seagulls
writing an epitaph in excrement above the coral
headstones, bleached. New Orleans always a sentence
away, always cheating the cyclopes of myth
each summer, the national weather service incessantly
renaming like some automaton Adam. Stay awake
is the hum of the mud. I can't decide which catfish
is frying, history or memory, in the skillet.

Iowa City Psalm

1.

Morning moves like the aging dancer
always imagined in cinema—backwards
and in the heels of fog.

A busker's yawn, arriving early, unpacks
an instrument of wrens,

a farmer's furrowed
boot alights in the market stall, granite

counters plead for a few coins, *another*
pivots on the lips of lovers—these liturgies

persist. Still, night has its hand
on the small of morning's back. See how
the rain doesn't reach it?

2.

By God, so much sky undressed?
Who knows where the chiffon of clouds has dropped.

What would lovers call themselves in this irresponsible
Midwestern light? No mountains passing judgment. Perhaps

the black robe of burned conifers would be too much. No
sea to speak incessantly. No endless summer, no invincibility.

Just this nonplussed light refusing to touch the strange
array of unbent wheat in a field. Is it too late

to learn defiance? To be less oblique? To sing into the head
of a sunflower as the bees do? Or am I still deciding

whether I deserved to be loved? All hum and no hymn.

3.

Midafternoon—the Midwest wants
to make everything plain, postcards instead of epistles,
the untouched bourbon remains on the windowsill,
shameless. Past glory becomes public memory. Still
all cottonmouth shy, all sly grin incandescent.

4.

If I enter the day late as the light,
the overcast, chalk-smear gray is broken
by a vulnerable blue. I am not
in awe as much as under an awning
of spent hope. An unfinished libretto.
Small-town life, please bring me some clarity,

seems to compose the muted chorus in
everyone's opera here. Song on song, lover
on a map and not in my bed, my name
on the cover of a book, but that book
in the discount bin, my heart, my heart,
lives like a wolf in a city alley:

everything out of place, everything
                      hungry, everything teeth.

5.

Is wonder the point? Does Adam, naming an animal, later say
but what do I mean by osprey?

The Silver Screen Asks, "What's Up Danger?" After We Enter

a lobby shaped like a yawn, lined with lodestone
leftover from making the marquee. The congress

of picture shows and pulp flicks it seems
named this movie house, the Senator.

Or maybe the city loves to signify. I guess
it matters little to a mill worker,

stevedore, or teamster how the name
came to be. My son and daughter

who will never walk home covered in soot,
longing for a moment in the mud room

to be responsible for nothing
but removing a coat, unlacing a boot,

my children slide like two slightly rusted magnets
toward the aluminum rail posts guarding

the popcorn counter. All the candy encased
in glass like masks in a museum. They've forgotten

our talk in the parking lot about Miles Morales,
about his animated face being so near to us

even without 3D, that this afro-latino Spider-man
could be our cousin, in a more marvelous universe.

But when they sit in the Senator's un-stadiumed
seats, with the ghosts of reel-to-reel clicking

their tongues, what I see on my children's faces
is not a season of phantasmal peace, but what's left

when the world's terrors retreat. Their whole brown
skin illuminated, like a trailer for another life.

Selena / Techno

Cumbia: spin, spin,
everlasting Tejano felicidades,
drop everything and twist, lift
both elbows and shame the whirlwind.
Head of a fan club. Vivas to those who have failed
to fathom a murderous love. Why did your name end
like a new moon? *Que hay unas personas
que no estan bailando*. What would the world be
if it had you instead of your legacy?

Urban Pastoral

Lent again in Baltimore: cigarettes stubbed out in the hand, gin locked in the liquor cabinet, bathroom scales reset to nil, under steamed mirrors. An Episcopal reverend is there on Harford and White Avenue in his eggshell frock, gripping a simple tin of ash. The laymen call him Father Tim. Afternoon is muting its trumpet of heat, and rush hour returns the employed to the neighborhood. Riffing, atonal. Few notice the folks gently tapping the air with gaunt fingers like a conductor. The sign of a cross town hack or a solicitation under the valve work of a traffic light. More see the slowing Chevys with open windows, foreheads pitched forward ready to receive the mark. Father Tim obliges, flicks a thumb through the car window, and soon the bus stop is all babble and queue as commuters catch on and step off the uptown express. Buildings this far north of the Inner Harbor are squat and dull, and so their shadows cup their hands in anticipation of night's black wafer, still hours away. Clouds kneel into color. Horizon pours its wine. Neighbors scratch meat from the grocery list and scratch their foreheads. Fish multiplies on the shelves, in the frying pans, as if to mimic the priest's banal liturgy, sizzling *and also with you*. This is the season where one thing becomes another. The body is lent a loaf of bread to break. The Reverend, thin as a piece of classroom chalk, closes his tin of ash to mark dusk. A firm hymn of gray hair plays on the scalp's pipe organs. A moan is on the stonework's lips, relentlessly porous and blued by patrol lights, the red giving up the ghost. Who hasn't wasted a beautiful gloam? Who hasn't been so archaic to think a black smudge and a blessing might work?

III | PIG-HEADED LIGHT

If faces were different when lit from above or below—what was a face? What was anything?

—William Golding, *Lord of the Flies*

The Beauty of Salt and Kitsch

A glutton's morning—the ten-minute storm apologizes
with peonies strewn across the veranda. Summer.

South of Ocean City, the unsheltered wild
horses are lifting their heads, their tails swatting

real and imagined flies. June bends a knee to Father's Day:
sub-eighties weather, an unmuted blue, the usual

sales at department stores. The NBA finals end
a game early. This is the last vacation before I turn forty,

and I don't bother with ocean sunrises or t-back
bikinis. The low tide of nearsightedness and middle age

has made room for other beauties. Two horseshoe crabs
tumble on shore still mating. An arcade of waves

returns them to the sea's discount ocean-view room but ends
their brief praise of the sun. Each sky-turned leg like a stylus

signing a letter to new heat. Along the boardwalk, I waste
money on mediocre pizza and watch my son tan like an Aztec.

The seagulls gut a fried Oreo and caw, triumphant. The afternoon
humidity is on a typical bender. We endure its stumbling gait—

my family, crazed suburban teens, out-of-state tourists, all
equal citizens in a democracy of sweat. Obvious and oblivious—brief

as my daughter's footprint on the sand—the daily rescues from riptide
the lifeguards perform. A swimmer's inertia as threat; the clouded sun

as inaccurate witness. We've come, willingly, to let kitsch
have its way with us. Double-decker tacos for lunch and Orange

Orange Crush for breakfast. Such are the marvels. Each hammock
swings between resignation and revelation. Salt is its own beatitude,

preserving a tradition of ordinary bliss: scuffs from a go-kart tire, the mini
golf's dogleg, the monogamy of takeout and a board game. Exquisite as working AC.

Apologia

The hydrangea unbuttons
a green blouse—oh Spring and its bruises

of sunlight that turn so vermillion
even breath could stain their skin.

In the stubborn clay, insatiable, sightless
worms perform their transubstantiation

through the fragile dark. The garden spade,
the beak of a sparrow, a child sheathing

a sword in the earth so it can be a stick again,
any of these interruptions.

Paradise Island

If the sea is illiterate, at least it speaks
                in two voices—its tidal baritone

saying *remember*; its high froth
                mumbling *forget*. The conch knows

it needs no wisdom from us, spiraling
                on and leaving a monument shell

with a listening gap. One day we will
                love as easily. But not today.

The sea swift sings a gull song
                as the waves flutter their blank pages

from the worn spine of horizon.

Post-Tenure

—For Kendra Kopelke and Steve Matanle and all teachers

All the anthologies have failed me, and the bookshelves rot. I search
them like a mirror searches a face, like a child thumbs a photo
album, for an echo of you. They are filled with your gifts
but not your names. These shelves can't remember you
better than I, and can't know what all teachers sacrifice
on the altars of time. What hymn would be enough,

what gentle accolade, what quiet monument for poets? The libraries
are filled with your students. The inner harbors of the mind are thick
with blackbirds. I say *Thank you*, and mean *Don't leave*, I mumble
gratitude, and mean *rescued*. Damn all the anthologies that ever were.
Damn their whispers. Damn the good night, the gentle, and the going.
Praise the play. Praise the heart's handmade book.

Nothing that's remembered ever retires, but praise the rest
and the restful. Praise Patience. Praise the carpe, the diem, and the ant.
Praise every way of looking. Praise the river moving
between now and another now and the stacks of books
we will walk through whispering, *teacher, teacher,*
where are you? Praise the silence as it slants and nods: *inside my life.*

Charismatic

—For Kyle Erickson

Remember Tulsa's tall grass full of spurs, & the Dodge
Caravan with a busted tape deck, how we pushed

that wood-paneled hunk of steel up a hill when the battery died?
Sisyphus. Somewhere in America, a person is writing a book

on the absurdity of friend making—form > function—when all
it took was a few fries and tenders and a few burning lungs

and, well, it was theater. There was such a year
of our Lord, right? When our childhoods weren't slain

in the spirit of evangelical mania. We had such a brief reprieve
before 9/11 and the towers fell into metaphor's incense. And even

longer before *The Speakerboxxx/The Love Below* would drop, blowing up
the swing of dance halls along Peoria Avenue. Midnight air stuck its thumb

in our mouths. I was used to catching the spirit, my whole body
a tambourine, and you watched *Breakin'* on the rabbit-ear

set in rural Oklahoma. Grove and groove. A bit of pop & lock, a bit of soul break
for the Nordic features your father lent you. Both our families reared

in Louisiana. *Cousin, Cousin* I might call out without error. What are the chances
we'd meet under the muddy foot of the American Plains. We panhandled a poor kid's cool

at a university built by a televangelist. No tithe like memory, eh? It was a healing
to make a friend so quickly, and it was a bit of acting

we studied and both abandoned to be poets. We remained in a *Twelfth Night*.
What good is any hindsight? Our regrets aren't any livelier than the dust-

filled drive-ins and remain thin as a fingernail. The same,
perhaps, for our spirited love. It's a shame that we can't go

back to those young men and tell them, like failed prophets: remember,
forgiveness isn't a stone, nor a beater van, nor a line drawn in the sand.

Mariah / Range

Stranded at the end of a high
note, quivering the diva's lips,
some A above high
C. The stratosphere & planets,
Heaven's ottomans, a note so high
the dogs bark in praise of a private
hearing. Such honey outside the hive,
such sweetness skimming
the humid air like a skiff.

Colonial Ledger

Some of us grew young with our tongue on the ocean
floor. Grounded in shoreline and oil. Pirogues raised
above our head like astonished eyebrows. The core
of the tide's accordion played with our feet. We did
not age. Smoked, salted folks nostalgic not for history's
art but for meat. Some of us knew the old beauties—
a stone fountain at the center of a garden, verandas
wearing the cool wig of the wind, the music in the last
room of a shotgun home. Common and sublime
as a Perley Thomas streetcar bell at dinnertime.

That fantasy of city we carried everywhere, some of us
aware we did not have the good sense to love
ourselves under the thumb of a FEMA claim. So, we ate
what we could cook and remember, we left the canoes
of youth to rot, we moved away, grew older and did not
age well. Some of us packed our accents in Foubough Tremé,
others escaped to a sister's place in Houston. Too many
made survivors where the Saints play. Some of us knew
and said nothing and were content with a laconic trumpet.

Ode to the Sword of Omens

I watched you, animated
                    seer without a Holy Spirit, no
humanity, just your whetted

steel-gray echoed in the morning fog
                    before kindergarten. My chin
rested in the chalice of my hands,

the ceremony of foil and antennae
                    was set, only a hard slap
could summon you from the cough of static.

Katoom. Katoom. Then an unsheathing
                    in song: Feel the magic, hear
the roar and you appeared slicing air.

That cat eye clouded with prophecy
                    and lodged in your hilt, widened
like a mailbox stuffed with debt letters.

Not even the clash and scrape
                    of a fork scrambling eggs
with rust in a worn pan, not even

the impatient stab of my mother's voice
                    could move me. In the living
room's predawn darkness

our oak-hued TV slung one soft orb
                    of light, washing my skin in RGB.
There were days I prayed to by high

yellow—how else would anyone know
                    I was beautiful. Sword of Omens

the lion-hero begged your hilt curve

like fang, like claw, like time;
                              grant sight beyond sight. It was a pleading
I recognized in my mother

every Sunday carrying a tenth of her
                              paycheck to the stage stairs
the preacher called altar.

What did she see turning back to her
                              pew, sweat swimming in the crest
of her finger waves? The steel gray

in every look that knew the amount
                              written was too quick to be anything
more than a widow's mite.

And I had a begging of my own
                              knowing my father was alive
circling our lives like a beltway

but not around, not sending out
                              a searchlight, like you
did every cartoon morning to call home

a squad of thunder. Sword of heroes,
                              what omens can you offer
that will sheathe the sadness

my mother wielded in a tithe?
                              Can you tell me how dark these steel
gray mornings will make my skin?

Can you tell me tomorrow's
                              weather? Can you tell me when
my father will come home again?

Precarious

Slick cherry boughs, labyrinthine
as steampunk pipework,

last night's rain and leftover
torrid odor on the breeze,

daylight and the moon are nude.
Baltimore's skyline smolders

like a rusted-through furnace
in an unfinished basement.

Against an anvil of light
a Black child strikes the empty

streets with a plain kickball
until morning is fully dressed

in a house-robe and slippers
of laughter. Would anyone argue

laughing alone
in the cool after dawn

isn't a stiff prayer,
as much as the first brushstroke

against primed canvas, or the pen-
ultimate hole rust eats

through a furnace?
And what of the industrious cherry

trees budding despite a summer
full of bullets to come?

Perhaps a bud is a minor
candle, lit on the boughs

which neither the breeze
nor the fog-colored waxwing

can snuff. Perhaps the blossom
imagines a people to come.

Splay Vespers Baltimore

In the typography of evening sky
helicopter floodlights dash out the stars

and swell the moon enough
dotting an end to October's unwieldy sentence

All hallows eve hangs like a hatchet
over firewood   each child

seeks mild horrors and wears them out
in public   A mask of moths

performs a danse macabre
around a crooked streetlamp

The bulb's filament and curved *come hither*
has them dead to rights

but no will for murder
or rather no means

this is a retelling of an old story

wish it for this city
with all the struck star's defiance

such pig-headed light
Eventually the moon bends

in ink like a partial thumbprint
or the cello's hips   Dead leaves form

serifs by which the wind is read
Some pumpkins slump

mere hours after the candles are snuffed
Everything enters the earth's subtext

without meaning
to   Dawn has rung out its dew-

drenched dishrag, so what mops
night's mud from the bootheels

of heaven seems superfluous
as any light postmortem   all saints

day turning with the tilling worms
all bodies return like poets

to a stone slate, seafoam, or a field of snow
torn costumes   flung on the floor

shredded like sea sending its tatters
to rain and rain and rain

countless ellipses that don't resolve.

Alla Prima Triptych*

Drawn. New Orleans, the end of Caribbean
sweat and the Mississippi's shivering. No more
numbering the things that cannot drown. Can find every island
and the land of the dead above a bar's threshold. Neon bleeding.

Drawn. Houston without jealousy calls itself a bayou
city. Rockets and wreckers clutch their screwtapes.
Slang every form of *slow, loud, and banging*. Every ward
a prime number. Can refugee. Endures the only season: humidity.

Drawn. Baltimore. Charm. An areola of accented vowels.
Dollar homes, rowhomes, vacants. Sandtown. Gray. Human
traffic. The Blue Nudes of Matisse. Snowballs in late summer.
12 o'clock at any hour of day. City Ouroboros. Moan and muscle.

*Exhibit Note: Every port town rhymes, like understudy and history, and so the artist must
post colonial. Call this canvas a bygone creolite or the pure pursuit of untitled negritude.
Every port town signifies on the great chain of the Atlantic. Dais and Diaspora.

ACKNOWLEDGMENTS

I would like to thank the following journals and anthologies in which these poems first appeared.

Smartish Pace: "A Poem Avoiding Its Own Tour of Force," "Early Morning Fade," "N.O. Star in Vinyl Overlay on a Drowned Living Room Floor," "Post-Tenure"

Scalawag: "Here Is a Sea We Cannot Call Sea"

The Hopkins Review: "THE UNITED FRUIT COMPANY," "Another Incident," "Halo," "Ode to the Sword of Omens," "Self-Portrait as Prince of the Fire Nation"

The Common: "Gorgoneion: Ft. Worth"

Brink!: "An American Sonnet for Johnson, VT," "Alla Prima Triptych," "Charismatic"

The Baffler: "A Perichoresis"

Bruiser: "Ode to Storm, Goddess, Thief, Mutant, Queen"

This Is What America Looks Like (Washington Writers' Publishing House): "Seasonal Depression"

The Future of Black (Blair): "Ode to Static"

The Quarry (Split This Rock): "The Silver Screen Asks, 'What's Up Danger' After We Enter"

Public School: "Paradise Island," "Self-Portrait in a Hand-Me-Down Shirt"

Strays: Strays from the Common Sense of Beauty (Foundlings Press): "The Beauty of Salt and Kitsch," "Ode to the Letter S," "The Beauty of the Galleria," "I Know You're Not a Pimp, But Pimp Remember What I Taught You," "Self-Portrait as Insect Song," "Colonial Ledger," and "Splay Vespers Baltimore"

Mid/South Sonnets (Belle Point Press): "Double Sonnet Instead of an Introduction"

There are many friends, compatriots, and colleagues I want to thank. Thank you Charif Shanahan for over a decade of true brotherhood. Thank you, always, zakia henderson-brown for being an embodiment of the common sense of beauty. Thank you, Kyle Erickson, for your compassion and vibrant living. Y'all are my spiritual siblings, the earliest to listen to what my poems were clamoring for.

I would not be a poet at all without the dedicated mentorship and teaching of Valzhyna Mort, Kendra Kopelke, Steve Matanle, and Tim Seibles. I live in endless gratitude to Cave Canem, the beloved community; may we keep, "signifyin' on the great chain of history."

I want to thank all the poets in Baltimore who have supported my work. Thank you, Dora Malech, for your excellent advice, your advocacy, and your friendship. Thank you, Tracy Dimond—long journeys make for long rewards. Tonee Mae Moll and Andrew Sargus Klein, thank you for being my accomplices against cruelty. Michael B. Tager, I am grateful for every collaboration, every dance, every conversation. Jalynn Harris, I can't wait to see what your poems become because of your faith in them. You inspire me. And to all the University of Baltimore Creative Writing and Publishing Arts MFA alumni, those who were my classmates and those who were my students, may a spirit of play always work its magic.

Thank you to my colleagues at the University of Baltimore, Marion Winik (much love, cousin!), Jane Delury, Betsy Boyd, Kyle Meikle, Jennie Keohane, Ian Power, and Rachael Zeleny. Each of you in large and small ways has enriched my intellectual life and thereby enriched this book.

Thank you Kara Duro for creating the captivating cover art. Each time I see it, I am touched by the texture of awe.

Though this is certain to be an incomplete litany, I want to thank Liz Hazen, Ann Marie Brokmeier, Joseph Ross, The Ivy Bookshop, Wildacres Writer's Workshop, *The Washington Independent Review of Books*, Gary Jackson, Len Lawson, Cynthia Manick, Ishion Hutchinson, Randon Billings Noble, Joseph Mills, Paisley Reckdal, Han VanderHart, Casie Dodd, C. T. Salazar, Karl Henzy, celeste doaks, HoCoPoLitSo, and Elizabeth Knapp.

This book could not have been written without the support of the Klein Family Foundation and its generosity toward the University of Baltimore. Some of the poems here were written while at the Vermont Studio Center. Some places such as Gillman School, Anne Arundel Community College, The Folger Shakespeare Library, Hood College allowed me to share these poems with audiences for the first time. I appreciate the support those institutions provided for me.

Though, "a brother is born for adversity," I am grateful to you, Rabu, for all the joy you've brought into my life. All we need is one of these books to hit it big and we can all quit our jobs. I appreciate all my cousins in New Orleans, the city of my birth, my Avalon, my second line at the end of the Mississippi, but particularly Shaun Coats. Thank you to my parents Rhonda Leyva and Carlos Leyva. I love you.

To my children, Simon and Tsunade, poetry pales in comparison to the music and laughter alive in you, but I hope this book is a testament to how our family chooses to love. Always choose love.

Lastly, to Casey, in the higher chorus of love, you are the octave of light that lingers.

NOTES

"A Poem Avoiding Its Own Tour of Force" uses several lines from "Lift Ev'ry Voice and Sing," a hymn originally written as a poem by James Weldon Johnson in 1899 and colloquially referred to as the Black National Anthem.

"Self-Portrait as Prince of the Fire Nation" takes its inspiration from Zuko, a character in the animated series *Avatar: The Last Airbender*.

"I Know You're Not a Pimp, But Pimp Remember What I Taught You" takes its title from a lyric in the song "Int'l Players Anthem (I Choose You)" by UGK ft. Outkast.

"Halo" references the title of "Let Me Clear My Throat," a song by DJ Kool.

"Ode to Storm, Goddess, Thief, Mutant, Queen" alludes to the Marvel character Ororo Munro, aka Storm of the X-Men. The poem also alludes to *Great Expectations* and *Oliver Twist* by Charles Dickens, albeit loosely.

"Ode to Static" pays homage to the character Static, created by Dwayne McDuffie. At the time of the character's debut in 1992, he represented one of the few Black superheroes created by a Black comic book creator.

"Early Sunlight, Broken Summer, Buttery Day" takes its title from a line in the poem, "One Turn Around the Sun," by Tim Seibles.

"Iowa City Psalm" alludes to a famous quote by Ginger Rogers about Fred Astaire, in which she said, "I did everything he did, but backwards and in heels."

"The Silver Screen Asks, 'What's Up Danger?' After We Enter" mentions the title of a poem by Derek Walcott in its penultimate couplet.

"Ode to the Sword of Omens" alludes to the one of the weapons wielded by Lion-O, the protagonist of the animated series *ThunderCats*.